I ATE ALL YOUR COOKIES

(and other things you wish you could tell your kids)

QUINN CONROY

 sourcebooks

Published by Sourcebooks, Inc.
P.O. Box 4410, Naperville, Illinois 60567-4410
(630) 961-3900
Fax: (630) 961-2168
www.sourcebooks.com

Library of Congress Cataloging-in-Publication data is on file with the publisher.

Printed and bound in the United States of America.

VP 10 9 8 7 6 5 4 3 2 1

INTRODUCTION

Sure, we love kids. They're cute. (*Ahem*, most of the time.) They have little chubby faces that beg to be smooshed. Or cleaned. It really all depends on the day. So yes, obviously we love them—we have wiped their butts after all, come on. But that doesn't mean we don't sometimes wish they were just a *little* smarter...or at least pretended to be smarter in public. Okay, maybe once in a while we think about admitting to them that we eat all the good stuff when they're asleep, just to see the pissed-off look on their face. Or we dream about telling them that *we* are the ones who filled their stockings with all that awesome stuff—so cool it on the whole "Santa rules" thing, because really, Santa sucks.

Of course we have these thoughts. And that's what *I Ate All Your Cookies* is all about. Laugh along with all the hilarious things you've ever wanted to say—but never will—to these relentless child overlords. What could be better therapy than laughing at them, all without their knowledge?

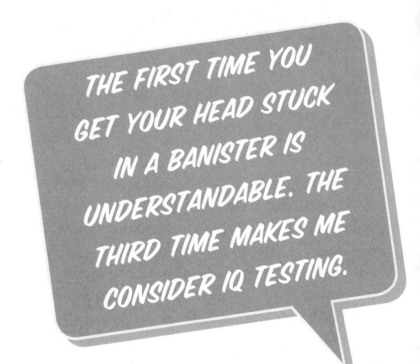

THE FIRST TIME YOU GET YOUR HEAD STUCK IN A BANISTER IS UNDERSTANDABLE. THE THIRD TIME MAKES ME CONSIDER IQ TESTING.

I AM MORE PROUD OF YOUR ABILITY TO BURP THE ALPHABET THAN ANY RIBBON OR TROPHY YOU COULD BRING HOME.

Your thinking face is a lot like your pooping face.

WHEN YOU TWIRL AROUND AND SAY, "ARE YOU WATCHING?" THE ANSWER IS USUALLY NO.

Your best friend is a twerp.
Let me be more specific.
He is clearly someone who
will live in his mother's
basement well into middle
age, watching pro wrestling,
eating only Hot Pockets,
and rarely bathing.
Mark my words.

I KNOW YOU'RE MISERABLE, BUT ITS TOTALLY WORTH IT. SUCK IT UP.

9

SOON, YOU'RE GOING TO LEARN HOW LITTLE I REALLY KNOW ABOUT PARENTING. I'M MAKING THIS CRAP UP AS I GO ALONG. DON'T TELL YOUR SISTER. SHE'S NEXT.

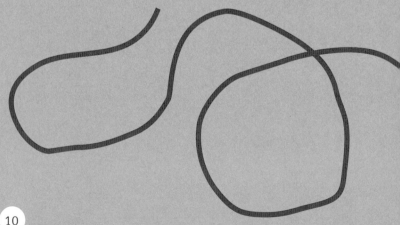

I'm not saying you were a practice kid, but I am saying that we plan on doing a much better job with the next one.

Oh, yeah, that baseball player is really big and strong. Let me tell you a little story about what steroids do to a person's "down there."

Yes, you're right.
Farts are
always funny.

I LIED. THE COOKIES
AREN'T ALL GONE. I'M
GOING TO EAT THEM
WHILE YOU'RE ASLEEP.
AND THEY'RE GOING TO
BE DELICIOUS.

I don't want to hear that Billy's mom did this, Billy's mom said that. It's time you learned that Billy's mom is an asshole.

YOU'VE BEEN RIGHT ALL THIS TIME. YOUR BROTHER <u>IS</u> MY FAVORITE CHILD.

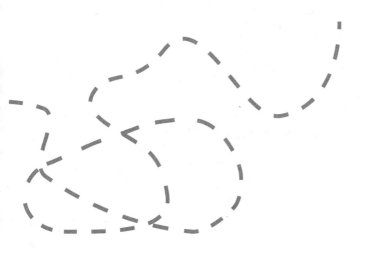

NO, THE DOG IS NOT ACTUALLY LIVING ON A FARM CHASING BUNNIES. AND THAT IS WHY THERE IS NO DIGGING ALLOWED IN THE BACKYARD.

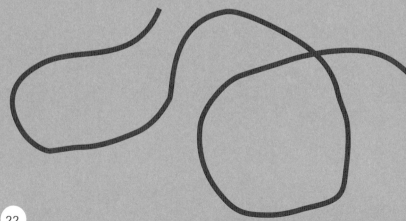

SOMETIMES IT'S OKAY
TO JUST BE AVERAGE.
AND YOU'RE IN LUCK—
I'M PRETTY SURE THAT
"AVERAGE" IS IN THE
CARDS FOR YOU.

The fact that you still eat glue makes me wonder if you're really as smart as I tell other people you are.

IT IS SO MUCH
EASIER TO LOVE
YOU WHEN YOU
ARE SLEEPING.

I almost always lie about the time so you have to go to bed earlier.

I KNOW THAT HITTING IS NOT ALLOWED, BLAH BLAH BLAH. BUT MAN, THAT STEVIE KID DESERVED IT. WHAT A LITTLE SHIT.

Yes, going to the dentist seriously *sucks*. Wait till you see the crazy sharp tools she's going to use, too. I would run if I were you.

IF I DON'T TALK TO SOMEONE BESIDES YOU TODAY, I MIGHT COMPLETELY LOSE MY MIND. YOU'RE NICE AND ALL, BUT YOU'RE A TERRIBLE CONVERSATIONALIST.

I WOULD LOVE TO LET YOU WATCH TV FOR HOURS ON END, BELIEVE ME. BUT I'M AFRAID THAT IF YOU ROT YOUR BRAIN, YOU'LL END UP LIVING HERE FOR TWENTY MORE YEARS. AND THAT IS JUST NOT HAPPENING.

I'm finally starting to realize the after effects of dropping you on your head.

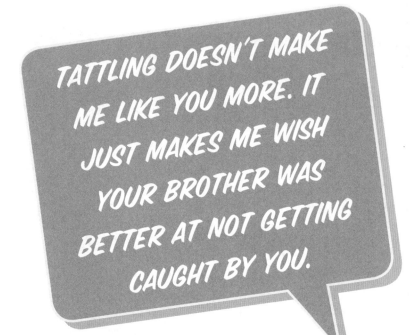

IT'S TRUE—YOU LOOK EXACTLY LIKE YOUR DADDY. I'M SO, SO SORRY ABOUT THAT.

WHEN I SAW YOU STICK
A DEAD ANT UP YOUR
NOSE AT THE PLAYGROUND,
I HAD THE SUDDEN URGE
TO TELL ALL THE OTHER
PARENTS THAT YOU
WERE ADOPTED.

The only reason we walk
to your karate lesson
is because Mrs. Johnson
brought a flask last time.
Meaning karate class
is now the happiest
of happy hours.

I promise never to dress you up like this again if you promise to stop sucking your thumb. You can't make that promise, can you? Deal's off!

YOU ARE THE
WORST BOWLER I
HAVE EVER SEEN.
I MEAN, REALLY.
THERE ARE FRICKIN'
BUMPERS.

IF THIS FAMILY WERE A REALITY SHOW, WE PROBABLY WOULD HAVE VOTED YOU OFF THE ISLAND SEVERAL EPISODES AGO.

Yes, I see you lost your two front teeth. You look completely ridiculous.

SOMETIMES I LIKE TO GET
YOU TO CRY JUST BEFORE THE
BABYSITTER COMES, SO I CAN
SEE THE HORRIFIED LOOK ON
HER FACE. PLUS, I LIKE TO
MAKE SURE I GET MY
MONEY'S WORTH!

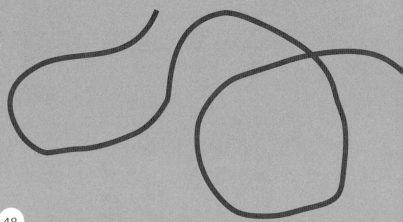

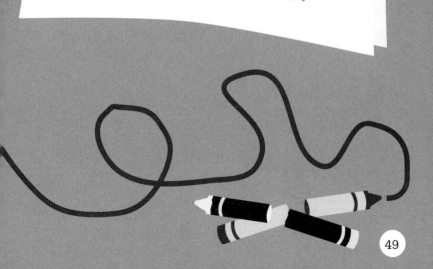

I'M NOT SAYING YOU WON'T MAKE IT IN COLLEGE. I'M JUST SAYING YOU SHOULD PROBABLY GET A JOB SO YOU CAN PAY SMARTER KIDS TO DO YOUR WORK FOR YOU.

YOU'RE THE REASON
I'M ON A FIRST-NAME
BASIS WITH THE LIQUOR
STORE CLERK.

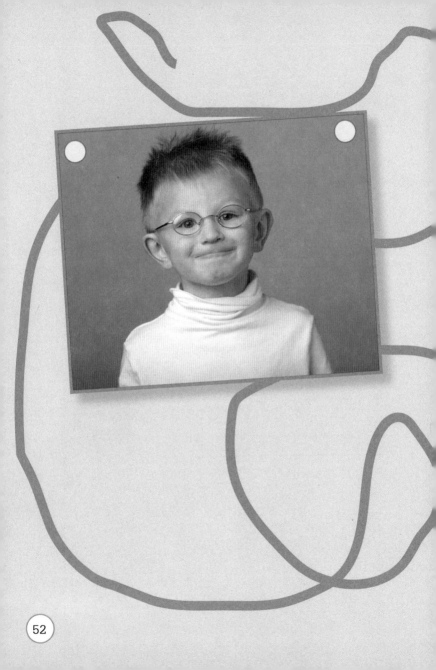

We think you're adorable, but oh, man, are the other kids going to pick on you.

It's your fault you're an only child. Maybe if you weren't so demanding, you'd have a baby brother or sister by now.

I actually can kick your ass at Candy Land. And checkers. And dominoes.

THE REASON THE
BEDSIDE DRAWER IS
LOCKED IS BECAUSE
MOMMY AND DADDY
HAVE THEIR OWN TOYS.

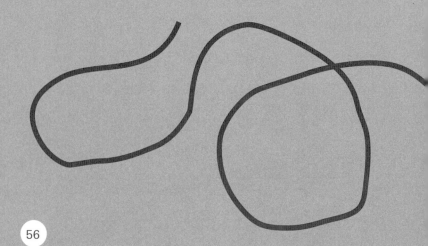

ABOUT SIXTY PERCENT OF YOUR HALLOWEEN CANDY ENDS UP IN MY BELLY ANY GIVEN YEAR.

I MIGHT BELIEVE THE INNOCENT ACT IF I HADN'T JUST SEEN YOU BITE YOUR BROTHER AND TRY TO PIN IT ON THE DOG. ACTUALLY, NO, NOT EVEN THEN.

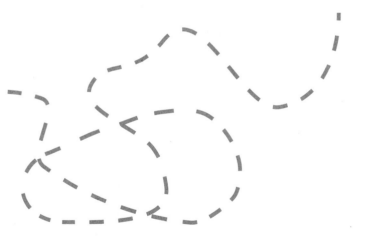

I'D LOVE TO TELL YOU THAT
YOUR BIRTH WAS SOME MAGICAL
EXPERIENCE, BUT REALLY, IT WAS
LIKE SOME SORT OF HORROR
MOVIE, FILLED WITH PAIN AND
SCREAMING AND LOTS OF GORE.
HOORAY!

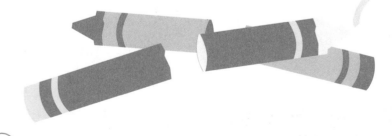

This is what my life has become. A series of soul-crushing questions:
(1) Why can't you ever flush the toilet?
(2) Do you ever chew the corn before swallowing it?

I'm sorry, sweetie, but expressions like this give me a glimpse into your future as a slack-jawed office drone.

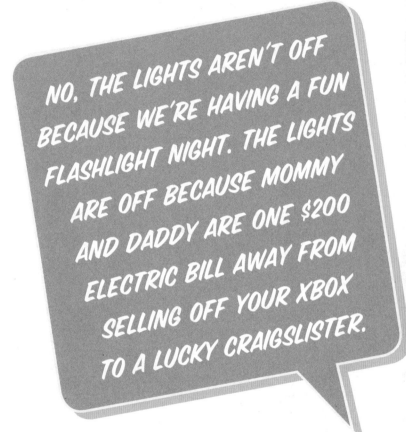

NOTHING IS
FUNNIER TO ME
THAN WHEN YOU
SWEAR.

If you fall asleep on there, I consider it permission to take enough photos to make you Facebook famous.

I do love you, but that doesn't mean I haven't considered trying to give you back to the hospital at least once.

I BLAME MY FARTS ON YOU WHENEVER POSSIBLE.

REMEMBER WHEN YOU THREW MY KEYS INTO THE TOILET AND THE CLICKER NEVER WORKED AGAIN? LET'S JUST SAY THAT MR. FLUFFY GOT A VERY SPECIAL TOILET-WATER BATH THAT DAY.

I KNOW YOU THINK
PANCAKES FOR DINNER
IS SUPER EXCITING,
BUT IT'S REALLY JUST
BECAUSE MOMMY
AND DADDY ARE LAZY
AS SHIT TODAY.

JUST ONCE, WHEN I HAVE TO RUN TO THE GROCERY STORE, I WISH I COULD KENNEL YOU WITH THE DOG INSTEAD OF TAKING YOU WITH ME.

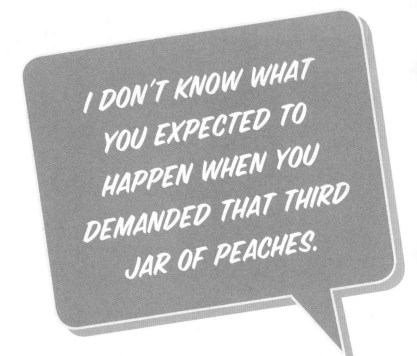

I LIED ABOUT ALWAYS HAVING ENOUGH DIAPERS IN THE HOUSE WHEN YOU WERE A BABY. YOU WERE TOTALLY WRAPPED IN PAPER TOWELS AT LEAST ONCE.

What do you mean you haven't had popcorn in forever? I just had some last night. Oh, that's right. I eat all the good stuff when you're asleep.

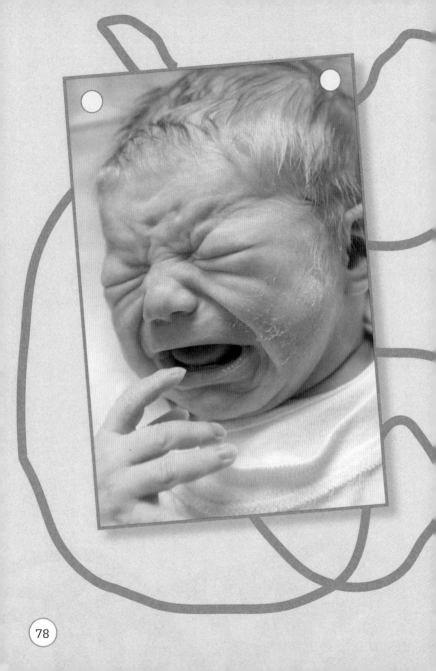

It's like reading tea leaves. I'm pretty sure your forehead wrinkles say, "Should have used a condom."

I'D BE HAPPY TO GET YOU WHATEVER IT IS YOU'RE ASKING FOR, BUT I CAN'T UNDERSTAND A DAMN THING YOU'RE SAYING SINCE YOU REFUSE TO LEARN HOW TO SPEAK CLEARLY.

I KNOW YOU'RE MY KID AND ALL, BUT SOMETIMES YOU ARE A TRULY DERANGED LITTLE WEIRDO.

I'M COUNTING DOWN
TO THE DAY WHEN YOU
STEAL YOUR FIRST CAR.
IT'S COMING—I FEEL
IT IN MY BONES.

Wait to crap your pants until I've handed you off to Uncle Paul next time, okay? He's been a total dick lately.

Clearly, one of you just relieved herself and the other was just a victim in all this.

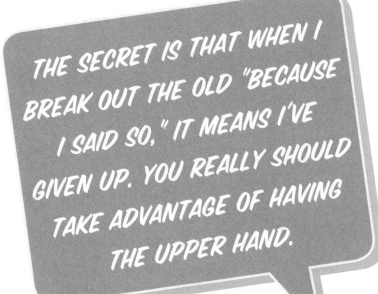

THE SECRET IS THAT WHEN I BREAK OUT THE OLD "BECAUSE I SAID SO," IT MEANS I'VE GIVEN UP. YOU REALLY SHOULD TAKE ADVANTAGE OF HAVING THE UPPER HAND.

I lied—the car radio isn't actually broken. But if I have to listen to Radio Disney for one more second, I will break all the speakers with a sledgehammer.

I'M ON TO YOU. I KNOW THAT SMILES LIKE THIS MEAN I CAN EXPECT TO FIND A TURD FLOATING IN YOUR BATH WATER TONIGHT.

I KNOW SOME PEOPLE SAY THEY LOVE THE SMELL OF THEIR BABY'S HEAD, BUT I REALLY HAVEN'T BEEN ABLE TO GET PAST THE WHOLE POOP-AND-PUKE THING YOU'VE GOT GOING ON.

I'M JEALOUS THAT YOU GET
TO STARE AT WEIRDOS, OPEN-
MOUTHED, BUT I'M SUPPOSED TO
POLITELY LOOK AWAY. I WANT
TO GAWK AT THAT CREEPY GUY
WITH THE PURPLE TRACK SUIT
AND NIPPLE CHAINS, TOO!

I WAS WONDERING WHY YOU SAID NO ONE AT SCHOOL SEEMED TO UNDERSTAND YOU. THEN I SAW YOU WALKING HOME BACKWARD, STOPPING SPORADICALLY TO CHASE BUTTERFLIES AND SNIFF YOUR ARMPITS. NOW I KNOW...YOU'RE _THAT_ KID.

WHEN YOU BRING HOME YOUR LATEST PAPIER-MÂCHÉ CREATION AND TELL ME YOUR TEACHER SAYS YOU HAVE "A LOT OF PROMISE," I HAVE TO WONDER WHERE IT IS HIDING.

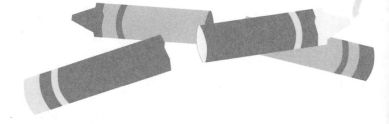

NOBODY WANTS TO SEE ALL THAT. GO PUT YOUR CLOTHES BACK ON.

Keep scowling. It's like seeing the sixty-year-old bald man you will someday be.

I'M NOT MAKING ANOTHER THING FOR A BAKE SALE UNTIL YOU LEARN TO POUR A GOOD, STIFF DRINK PROPERLY. HOW MANY TIMES DO I HAVE TO TELL YOU TO GO EASY ON THE CLUB SODA?

GETTING SHOTS AT THE DOCTOR IS SCARY AS SHIT. YOU ARE TOTALLY RIGHT TO FREAK OUT.

When you were first born, I wasn't sure if I could love you as much as I love the dog. I totally do! But it was a toss-up there for a little while.

I THREW OUT THAT MACARONI THING YOU DID LAST WEEK, AND I'M GOING TO THROW OUT THE NEXT ONE, TOO. SIX AWFUL PIECES OF ART ARE QUITE ENOUGH FOR THE FRIDGE.

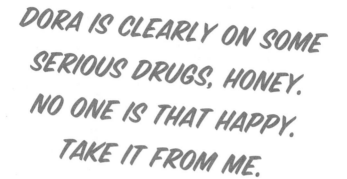

DORA IS CLEARLY ON SOME SERIOUS DRUGS, HONEY. NO ONE IS THAT HAPPY. TAKE IT FROM ME.

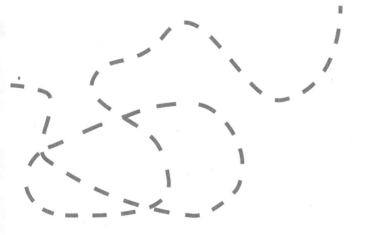

If you don't stop with the public tantrums, I'm going to tell you where you really came from. And show you the video.

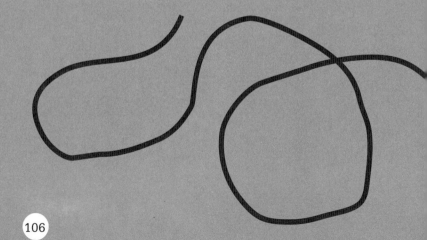

THE SECRET IS THAT GROUNDING YOU DOESN'T MEAN ANYTHING. IF YOU JUST SHUT YOUR TRAP FOR A COUPLE OF DAYS, I'M GOING TO FORGET THAT I SAID "NO TV FOR A MONTH."

Oh, no. I just realized I've spawned the kind of kid that steals other kids' lunch money. Time to start saving for that first bail.

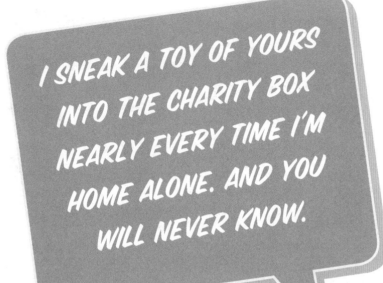

I CAN'T WAIT UNTIL YOUR FACE FINALLY GROWS INTO THOSE GIANT TEETH. YOU SORT OF _DO_ LOOK LIKE A RABBIT.

No, you're not getting a pet. I just watched you lick a toenail clipping you found on the bathroom floor.

THOSE PRINCESS TATTOOS COVERING YOUR ARMS FREAK ME OUT—I KEEP IMAGINING YOU AS THE HEAD OF A VERY FRILLY BIKER GANG, ONE THAT DOESN'T KNOW HOW TO SHARE AND ALWAYS DEMANDS FRUIT SNACKS.

COULD YOU TRY NOT TO CHEW YOUR GUM LIKE A COW CHEWING CUD? YOU'RE STARTING TO DROOL. MORE IMPORTANTLY, YOU'RE EMBARRASSING ME.

Yep, you're super, all right. Super good at pissing the bed every other night.

That letter from Santa telling you to start making my coffee in the morning? Yeah, I wrote that.

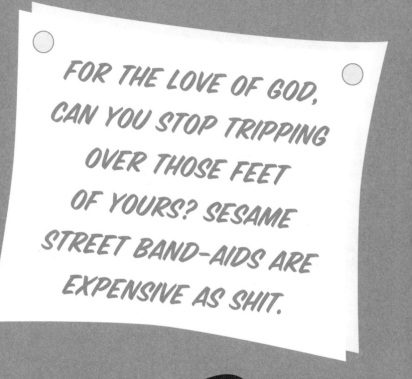

FOR THE LOVE OF GOD, CAN YOU STOP TRIPPING OVER THOSE FEET OF YOURS? SESAME STREET BAND-AIDS ARE EXPENSIVE AS SHIT.

No, you probably don't need that many layers. But I wanted to see if I could get your arms to stick straight out like Randy in A Christmas Story.

Of course Mommy and Daddy share—we share a Xanax before each and every school concert to dull the pain.

YOU KNOW THAT I SKIP AT LEAST FOUR PAGES EVERY TIME I READ YOU A BEDTIME STORY, RIGHT?

It's times like this when I wish I could pretend you're not mine.

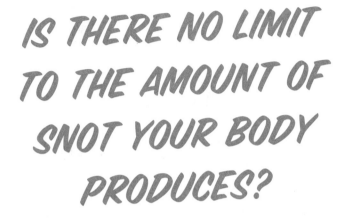

IS THERE NO LIMIT TO THE AMOUNT OF SNOT YOUR BODY PRODUCES?

OF COURSE I HAVE TO
TELL YOU JUST TO IGNORE
BULLIES. BUT REALLY, NOTHING
SHUTS THEM UP FASTER THAN A
SWIFT PUNCH TO THE CROTCH.

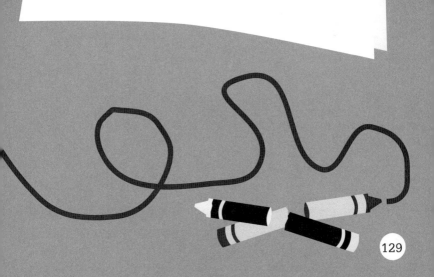

129

I'M SO PISSED OFF THAT YOU WERE SWEARING AT SCHOOL, BUT ONLY BECAUSE I HAVE TO WATCH MY DAMN MOUTH WHEN I'M AROUND YOU NOW.

WHEN AUNT LINDA BRAGS ABOUT YOUR COUSIN SKIPPING A GRADE, I DO FEEL A LITTLE JEALOUS. YESTERDAY YOU WENT OUTSIDE FOR TEN _SECONDS_ AND CAME BACK WITH YOUR CHIN COVERED IN MUD, YOUR SHOES MISSING, AND A DEAD BIRD IN YOUR POCKET. _TEN_ _SECONDS!_

Your laugh gets decidedly more evil-sounding when you've had sugar. I'm talking sociopath-quality.

When my boss was visiting and you yelled, "Someone wipe my butt!" down the stairs? Yeah, not your best moment.

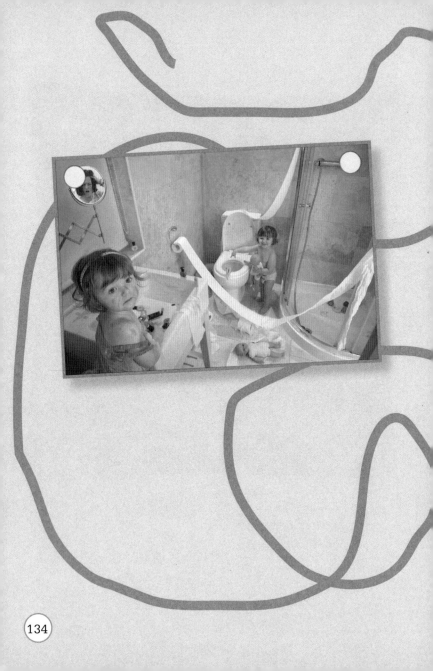

It's times like this when I realize I am never, ever going to agree to have another child.

LYING ON THE FLOOR SCREAMING YOUR DAMN HEAD OFF WILL NOT ENTICE ME TO LET YOU HAVE A SLEEPOVER. DO YOU REALLY THINK I WANT FIVE MORE OF YOU LITTLE ASSHOLES AROUND HERE?

I LOVE YOU, BUT NO, I DON'T THINK YOU'RE REALLY GOING TO BE AN ASTRONAUT.

I know, I know, that sweater is awful. But Aunt Gertrude expects to see it on you, and the bitch holds a grudge.

OUT OF THE MANY LIES
I'VE TOLD YOU, THE
USEFULNESS OF MATH IS
PROBABLY THE BIGGEST.

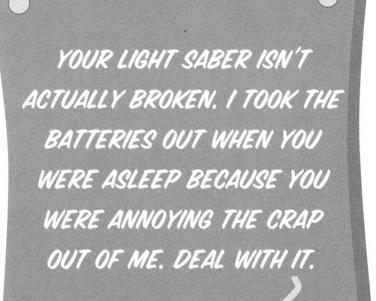

YOUR LIGHT SABER ISN'T ACTUALLY BROKEN. I TOOK THE BATTERIES OUT WHEN YOU WERE ASLEEP BECAUSE YOU WERE ANNOYING THE CRAP OUT OF ME. DEAL WITH IT.

You do realize that Elmo has a hand up his butt, right?

YOU'RE SO RIGHT. BRUSSELS SPROUTS ARE DISGUSTING. THEY'RE LIKE GIANT, ROUND, GREEN BOOGERS. BUT THE GREAT PART ABOUT BEING A GROWNUP IS THAT I'M SURE AS HELL NOT GOING TO EAT THEM...BUT YOU ARE!

I'M AFRAID YOU'RE NOT THE SHARPEST TOOL IN THE SHED. YOU ONCE HID A POTATO UNDER YOUR PILLOW AND TRIED TO FEED IT BECAUSE YOU THOUGHT IT LOOKED LIKE GRANDPA.

Yes, I knew that a taste of buttermilk might lead to projectile vomit. That's why I aimed you toward Uncle Howard's horrible new tie.

I USED YOUR BEDWETTING TO GET OUT OF A PLAYDATE WITH THE GREERS. SO, IF YOU SEE THAT KID TOMMY, ACT TIRED. AND IF HE POINTS AND LAUGHS...YOU KNOW WHY.

Yes, I know exactly when you're lying. But that doesn't mean I always care.

It wasn't the Tooth Fairy who was incredibly cheap. It was me! Honey, you're seriously overestimating the value of that grody-ass tooth.

I WOULD TELL YOU TO STOP
KICKING THAT GUY'S SEAT,
BUT HE TOTALLY JUST
YELLED AT THE FLIGHT
ATTENDANT AND IS OBVIOUSLY
A DICK. SO...KICK AWAY!

YES, I'M AWARE THAT YOUR SNOOPING IN MY UNDERWEAR DRAWER WILL MEAN THERAPY LATER ON IN LIFE. GOOD LUCK WITH THAT.

I bet any money that this thing will be covered with your disgusting, slimy slobber within ten seconds.

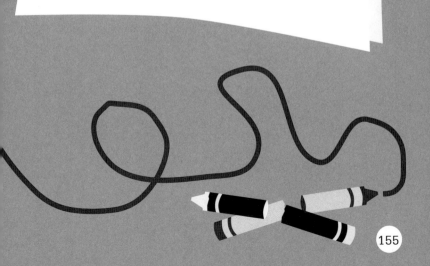

LITTLE CINDY GAVE YOU A VALENTINE, HUH? DID SHE EXPLAIN EXACTLY WHAT SHE SAW IN YOU?

AT THE TIME, I SCOLDED YOU. BUT WHEN YOU SAID "POOPING IS AWESOME!" IN THE MALL BATHROOM, I REALLY HAD TO AGREE.

Release that poor man! I hate to break it to you, but he ain't magic. If Santa were real, do you think he'd smell so clearly of whiskey and menthol cigarettes?

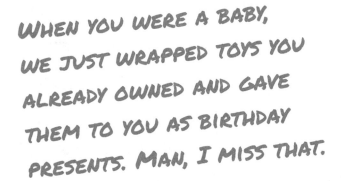

WHEN YOU WERE A BABY, WE JUST WRAPPED TOYS YOU ALREADY OWNED AND GAVE THEM TO YOU AS BIRTHDAY PRESENTS. MAN, I MISS THAT.

I ADMIT IT:
I'M JEALOUS THAT PANTS
ARE OPTIONAL FOR YOU.

No, Mommy and Daddy weren't actually wrestling when you walked in without knocking.

I'M NOT LOOKING FORWARD TO YOU
JOINING FACEBOOK OR TWITTER.
I'LL HAVE TO GO BACK AND DELETE
ALL THE EMBARRASSING THINGS
ABOUT YOU THAT I SHARED WITH
THE WORLD...LIKE WHEN YOU GOT
US KICKED OUT OF THE STORE FOR
PLAYING WITH YOURSELF IN
THE PRODUCE AISLE.

NO, YOU CAN'T HAVE A GERMAN
SHEPHERD. NO ONE SHOULD HAVE
A PET SMARTER THAN THEY ARE.

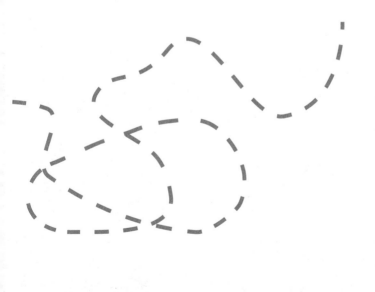

Your resemblance to a hungover Rush Limbaugh is really starting to freak me out.

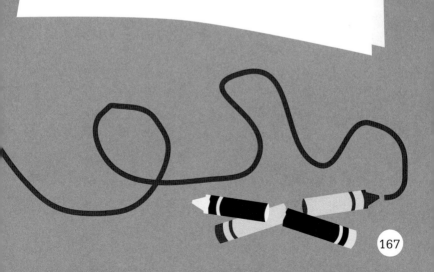

I HAVE TO TRY REALLY HARD NOT TO GET OFFENDED WHEN PEOPLE SAY YOU LOOK JUST LIKE ME.

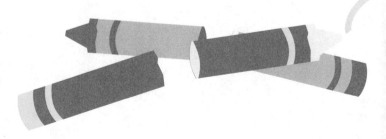

You know how you fart in your sleep? Well, let's just say that after the one millionth view, you are now officially Internet famous.

YOUR MUSIC IS AN UNDISCOVERED INSTRUMENT OF TORTURE. WHEN YOU'RE THIRTY, I'M GOING TO PLAY KIDZBOP NONSTOP IN YOUR EARS AND SEE HOW WELL YOU HOLD UP.

I'll still love you when you're the socially awkward teenager who corrects the grammar on his classmates' tweets. I'm just not sure they will.

THERE'S SOMETHING I'VE
BEEN MEANING TO TELL YOU:
YOU LOOK REALLY DUMB
WHEN YOU CRY.

WHEN I TELL YOU HOW PROUD I AM THAT YOU POOPED IN THE TOILET, WHAT I'M REALLY THINKING IS: "WHEN IN THE HELL WILL YOU LEARN TO WIPE YOURSELF ALREADY?"

IF I FIND ONE MORE
BOOGER WIPED ONTO
A WALL, YOU'RE GOING TO
BE WEARING MITTENS
YEAR-ROUND.

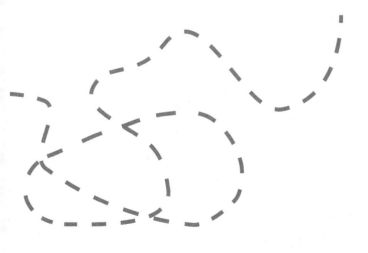

YOU ARE BASICALLY UNINTELLIGIBLE EIGHTY PERCENT OF THE TIME, BUT THAT DOESN'T MEAN I WANT YOU TO REPEAT YOURSELF.

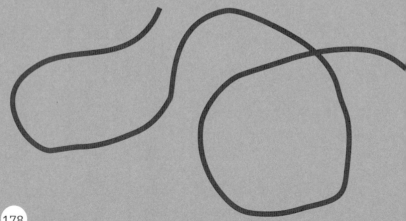

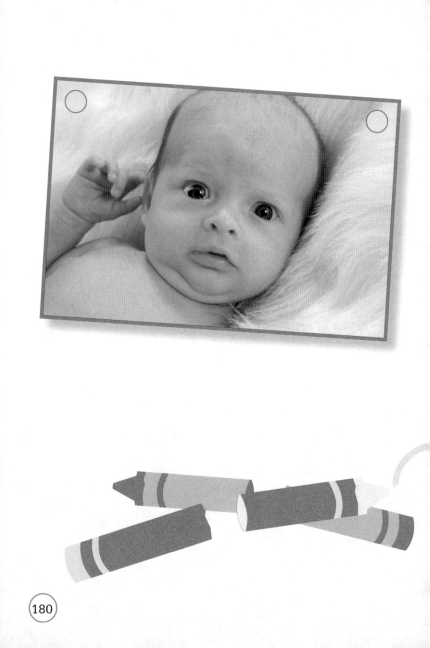

Now you're all cleaned off and cute-like, but <u>damn</u>, you were gross-looking when you first came out.

IT'S OKAY THAT YOU'RE NOT THE SMARTEST, HONEY. YOU'RE CUTE. YOU CAN MARRY A SMART GIRL WHEN YOU'RE OLDER WHO CAN DO ALL YOUR THINKING FOR YOU.

I GENERALLY STOP LISTENING TO YOU TELL ME ABOUT YOUR DAY AFTER THIRTY SECONDS OF "AND THEN WE DREW SHAPES AND THEN..."

The only thing worse than the sound of you singing is the sound of you singing in unison with others just like you.

REALLY? AGAIN? HOW HARD IS AN ESCALATOR? FIGURE IT OUT.

My first clue that your teacher doesn't like you? The stack of military school brochures she handed me at parent-teacher night.

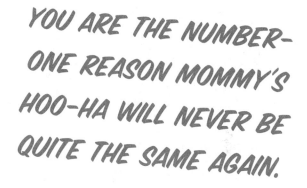

YOU ARE THE NUMBER-ONE REASON MOMMY'S HOO-HA WILL NEVER BE QUITE THE SAME AGAIN.

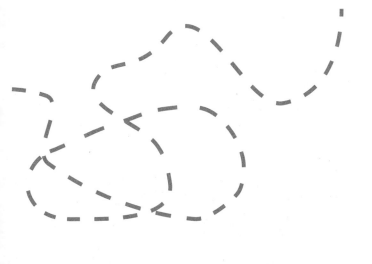

I WOULD GO TO THE ZOO EVEN IF I DIDN'T HAVE YOU. BUT THANKS FOR GIVING ME A GOOD COVER STORY. IN RETURN, YOU CAN HAVE A SNOW CONE, EVEN THOUGH IT COST TWENTY CENTS FOR THE ICE AND FIFTEEN DOLLARS FOR BEING INSIDE ZOO PROPERTY.

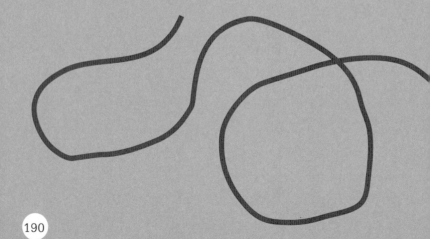

191

Yeah, you better start saving. Because when I'm in diapers, it's payback time. You're going to need to hire some extra help.

LET'S FACE IT—I'M NOT A PERFECT PARENT. BUT YOU'RE NOT A PERFECT KID, SO IT'S ALL GOOD.

I DON'T REALLY REMEMBER
WHAT EIGHT HOURS OF SLEEP
FELT LIKE. AND I ONLY HAVE
YOU TO BLAME.

Payback will come, my dear. I have a list of things I'm going to tell your first boyfriend. #1: the time you got naked at Aunt Molly's wedding ceremony and peed on her dress. In church.

Huh. Who knew?
Sugar crashes make
you look <u>exactly</u>
like a deranged
sea monster.

OKAY, SO YOU'RE NOT REALLY ALLERGIC TO APRICOTS. IT'S JUST THAT YOU LOVED THEM SO MUCH AS A LITTLE KID, IT WREAKED HAVOC ON OUR PLUMBING.

The first thing I'm going to teach you when you learn to drive is how to properly flip someone off while simultaneously honking.

ACKNOWLEDGMENTS

A lot of unvented sarcasm and hostility went into the making of this book. Many thanks to Philip, Shana, Tina, Patrick, Kelly B., Greg, Kay, Krista Joy, Kelly B.S., Heather, and Sarah for sharing their hidden (and not-so-hidden) dark sides. And, of course, much appreciation to the child overlords who are the inspiration for so many deep-seeded feelings. Good luck, kids, when you (*gulp*) take over the world for real one of these days. Well, really, good luck to us all when that happens.